FRENCH-ENGLISH
WORD PUZZLE BOOK

Catherine Bruzzone, Rachel Croxon and Louise Millar

Illustrations by Louise Comfort and Steph Dix
French adviser: Marie-Thérèse Bougard

BARRON'S

À la ferme

Complète les mots. Ensuite fais les mots croisés et vérifie les réponses à la page 30.

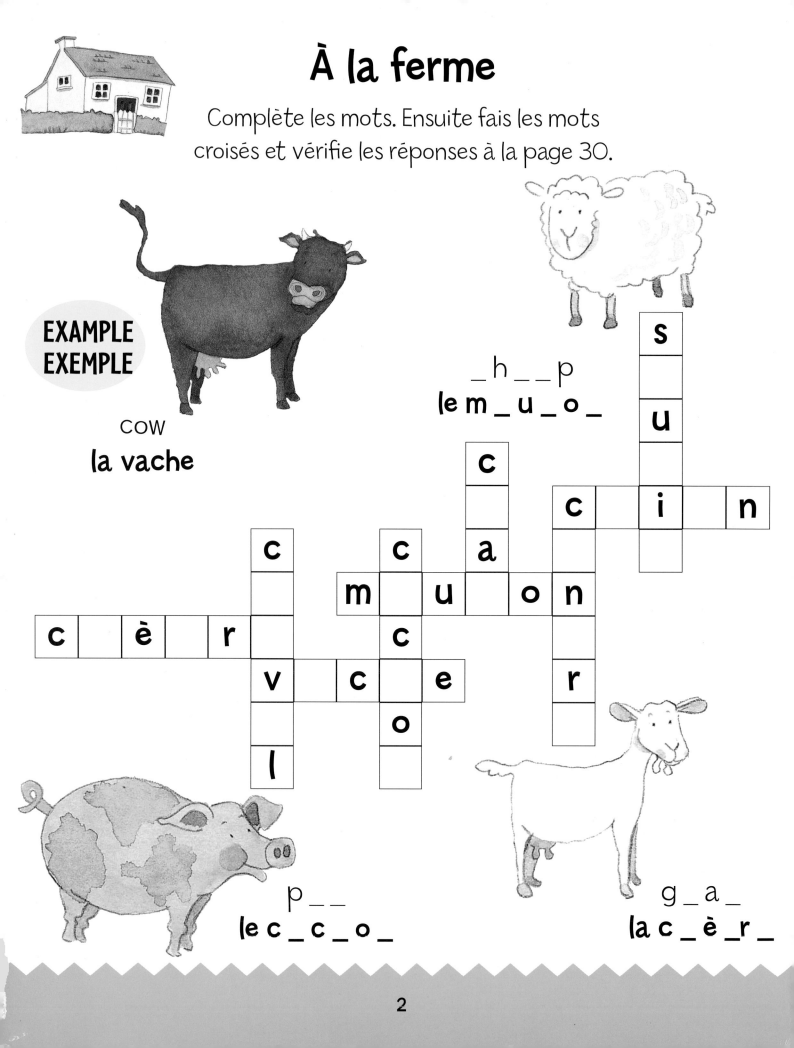

EXAMPLE
EXEMPLE

cow
la vache

_ h _ _ p
le m _ u _ o _

p _ _
le c _ c _ o _

g _ a _
la c _ è _ r _

On the farm

Label the pictures. Then fill in the crossword and check your answers on page 30.

c _ _
le c _ a _

m _ _ s_
la s _ u _ i _

h _ r _ _
le c _ e _ a _

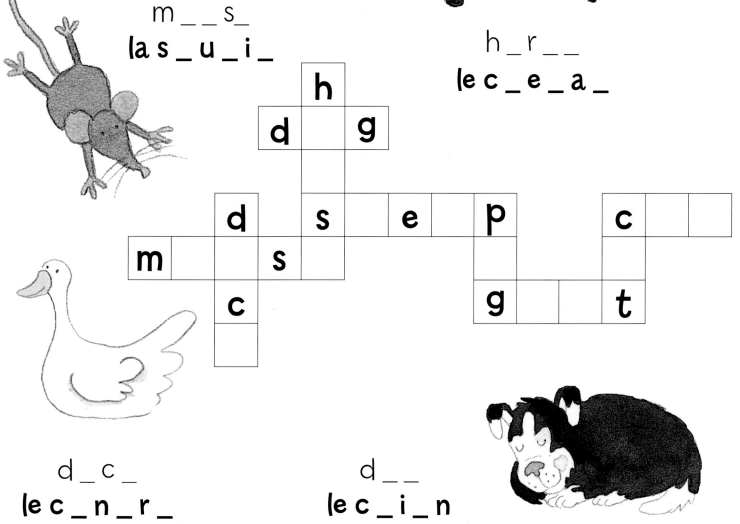

d _ c _
le c _ n _ r _

d _ _
le c _ i _ n

Le supermarché

Complète les mots. Ensuite trouve ces neuf mots dans la grille. Solutions à la page 30.

EXAMPLE
EXEMPLE

egg   l'œuf   b_e_d   le p_i_

m_l_
le l_i_

v	a	b	h	x	p	a	i	n	w
o	e	u	f	a	m	l	d	s	r
w	t	h	m	v	x	o	a	t	i
p	o	i	s	s	o	n	s	d	z
â	t	b	a	u	l	v	x	o	a
t	x	l	d	c	b	l	a	i	t
e	h	w	s	r	a	w	o	h	b
s	b	v	b	e	u	r	r	e	t
l	o	d	w	b	d	x	s	l	v
t	h	a	v	i	a	n	d	e	x

b_tt_r

le b_ _rr_

f_s_

le p_ _ss_n

4

The supermarket

Label the pictures and then look for the nine words in this square. Answers on page 30.

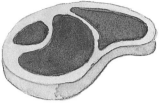

m _ a _
la v_ a _ d _

p _ s _ a
les p â _ e _

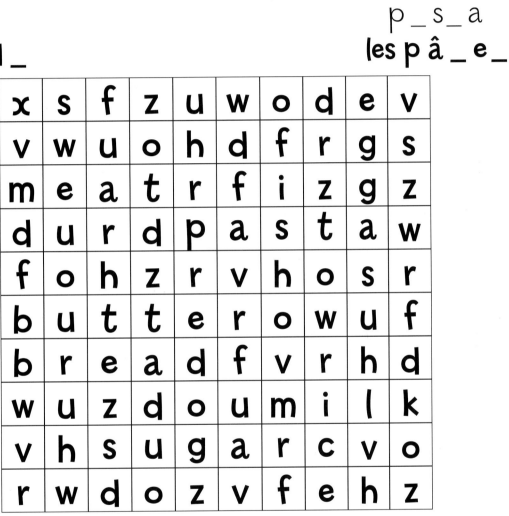

x	s	f	z	u	w	o	d	e	v
v	w	u	o	h	d	f	r	g	s
m	e	a	t	r	f	i	z	g	z
d	u	r	d	p	a	s	t	a	w
f	o	h	z	r	v	h	o	s	r
b	u	t	t	e	r	o	w	u	f
b	r	e	a	d	f	v	r	h	d
w	u	z	d	o	u	m	i	l	k
v	h	s	u	g	a	r	c	v	o
r	w	d	o	z	v	f	e	h	z

s _ g _ r
le s _ c _ e

r _ c _
le r _ z

Qu'est-ce que c'est?

Relie les points et complète le nom de ces créatures. Solutions à la page 30.

EXAMPLE
EXEMPLE

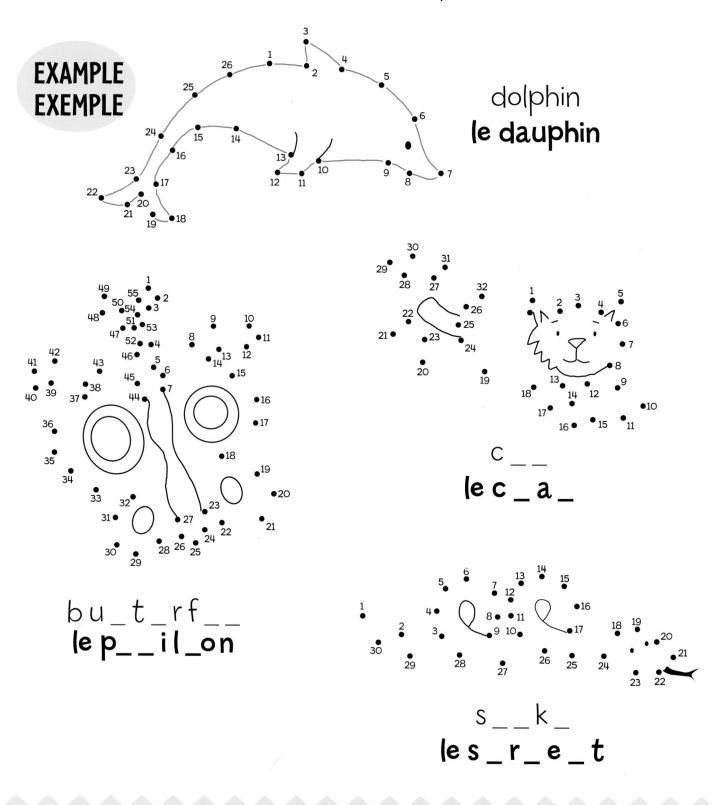

dolphin
le dauphin

b u _ t _ r f _ _
le p _ _ i l _ on

c _ _
le c _ a _

s _ _ k _
le s _ r _ e _ t

6

What is it?

Join the dots and complete the names
of these creatures. Answers on page 30.

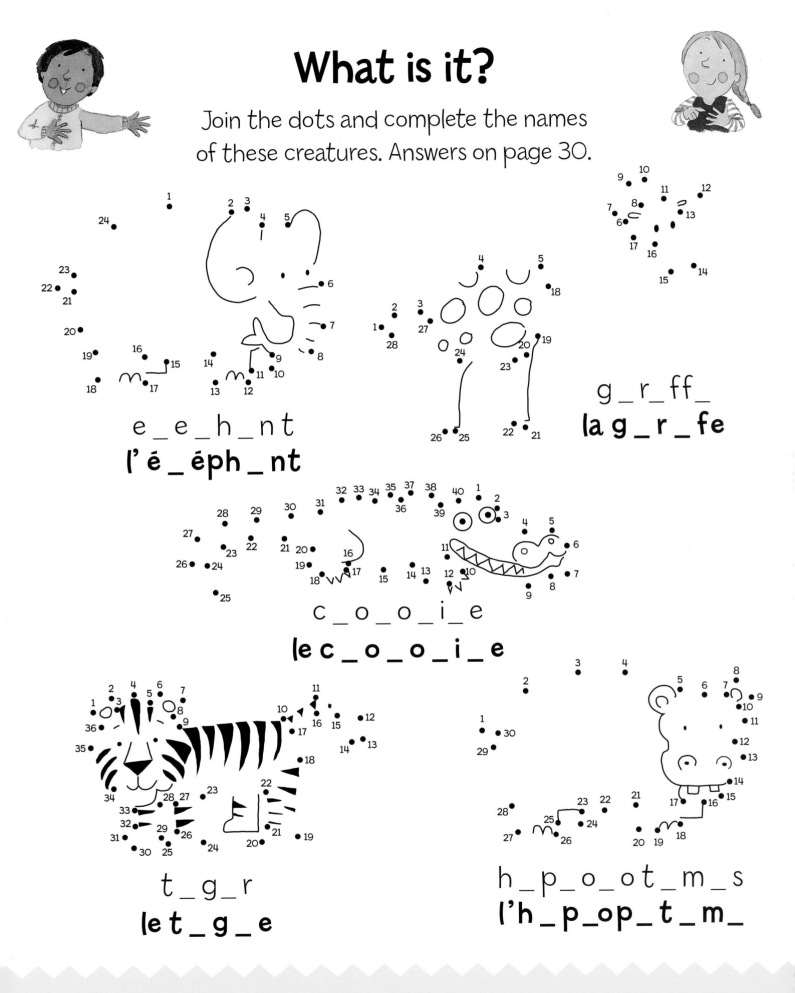

e _ e _ h _ n t
l' é _ éph _ nt

g _ r _ ff _
la g _ r _ fe

c _ o _ o _ i _ e
le c _ o _ o _ i _ e

t _ g _ r
le t _ g _ e

h _ p _ o _ o t _ m _ s
l' h _ p _ op _ t _ m _

Dans la cuisine

Complète les mots. Utilise les lettres entourées pour former le mot qui manque en bas de la page. Solutions à la page 30.

s☐nk
l'é_i☐r

s_u_ep_n
la ☐asse_ole

s_ _o☐
la c☐illèr_

☐ri_ge
le frig☐

le | | | | | | |

In the kitchen

Fill in the missing letters of the labels. The letters in boxes make up the final missing word below. Answers on page 30.

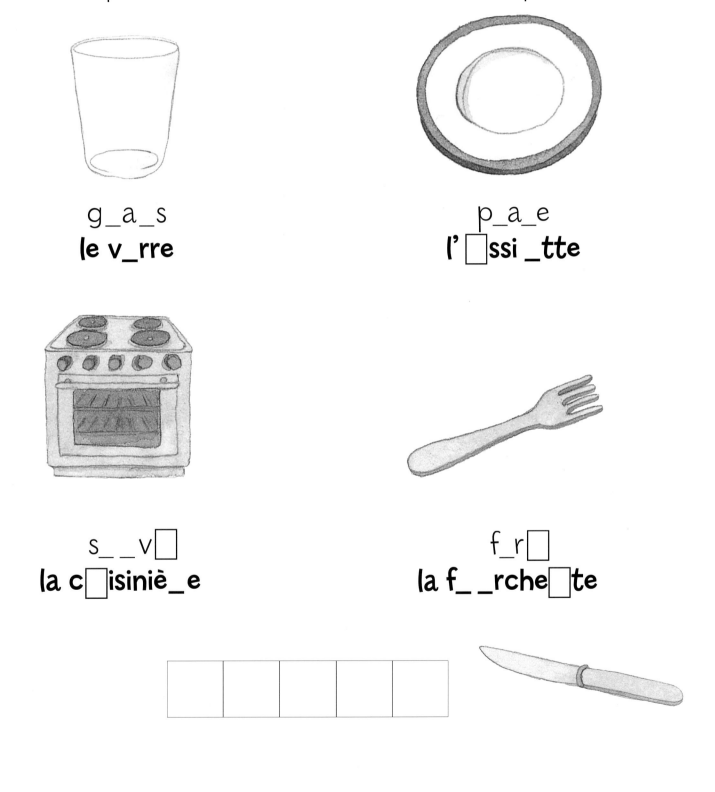

g _ a _ s
le v_rre

p _ a _ e
l' ☐ssi _tte

s_ _ v☐
la c☐isiniè_e

f_r☐
la f_ _rche☐te

Les couleurs de l'arc-en-ciel

Complète les mots. Ensuite fais les mots croisés.
Vérifie les réponses à la page 30.

EXAMPLE
EXEMPLE

green **vert**

b _ a _ _   n _ i _

b _ u _
b _ e _

o _ _ n _ _   o _ a _ _ _

Colors of the rainbow

Label the pictures. Then fill in the crossword and check your answers on page 30.

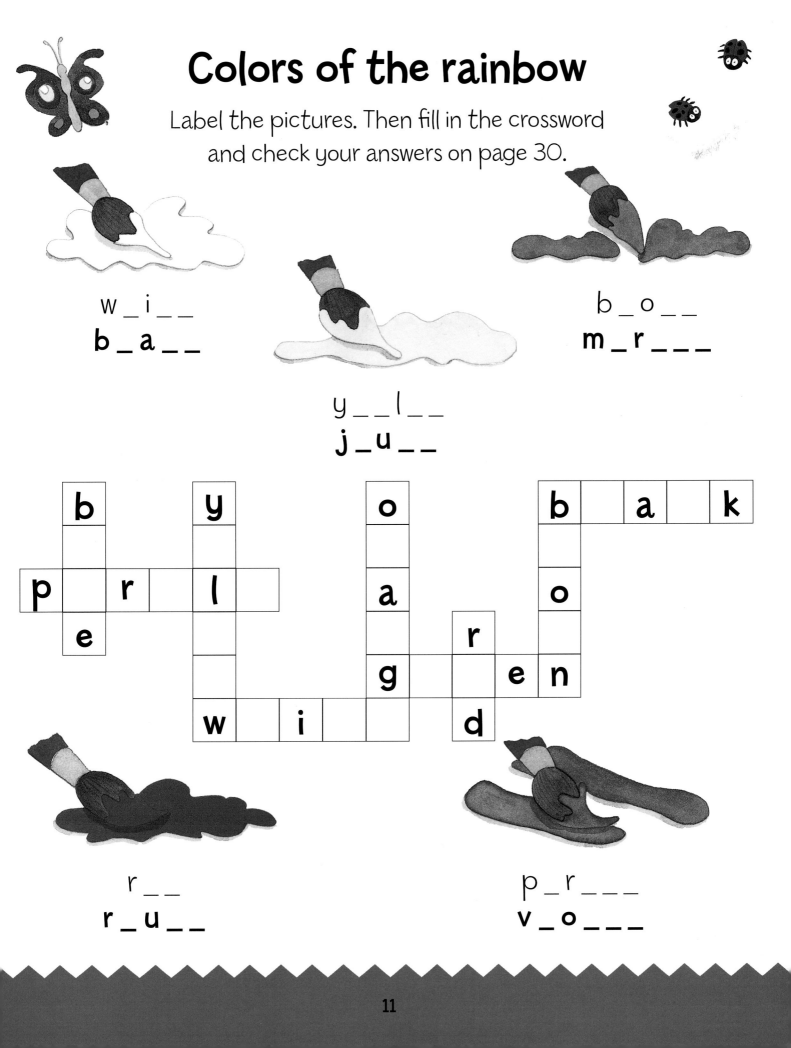

w _ i _ _
b _ a _ _

y _ _ l _ _
j _ u _ _

b _ o _ _
m _ r _ _ _

b		y			o			b		a		k
p	r		l			a				o			
e							r							
						g		r	e	n			
w	i				d								

r _ _
r _ u _ _

p _ r _ _ _
v _ o _ _ _

Le marché

On a mélangé le nom des fruits.
Complète les mots sous chaque corbeille de fruits.
Solutions à la page 30.

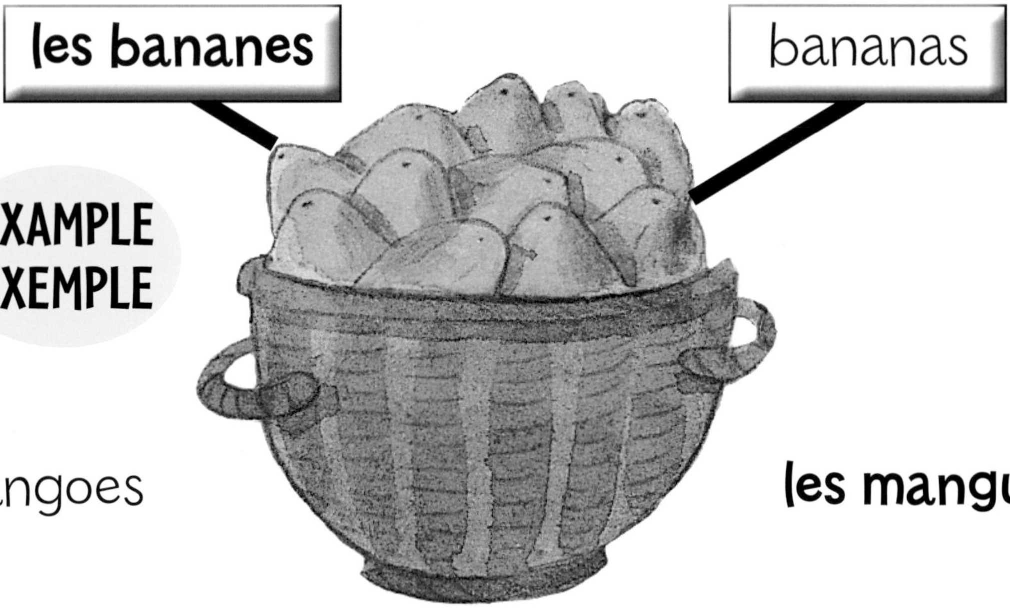

les bananes

bananas

EXAMPLE
EXEMPLE

mangoes

les mangues

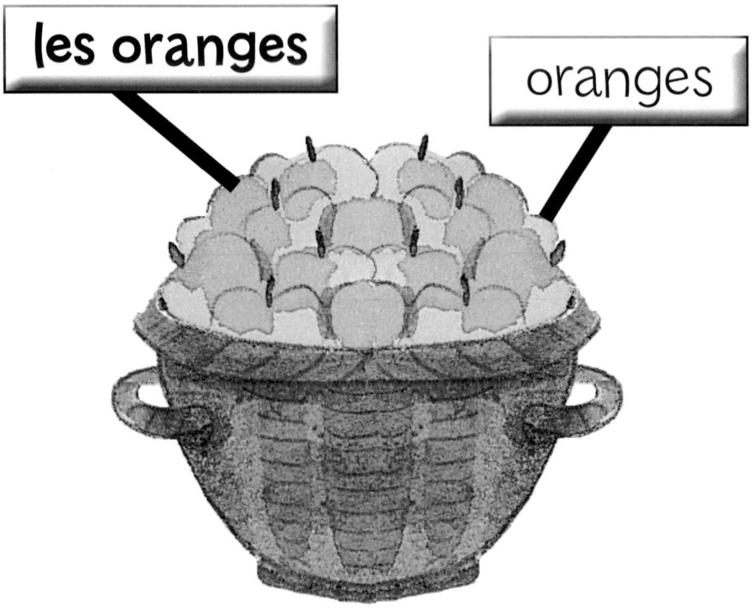

les oranges

oranges

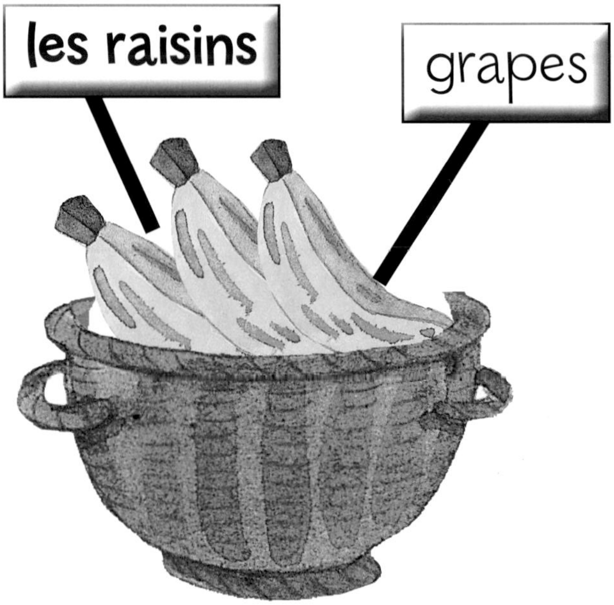

les raisins

grapes

les _ _ _ _ _ _ _

les _ _ _ _ _ _ _

The market

Someone has mixed up the labels on the fruit.
Can you write the correct names under each basket of fruit?
Answers on page 30.

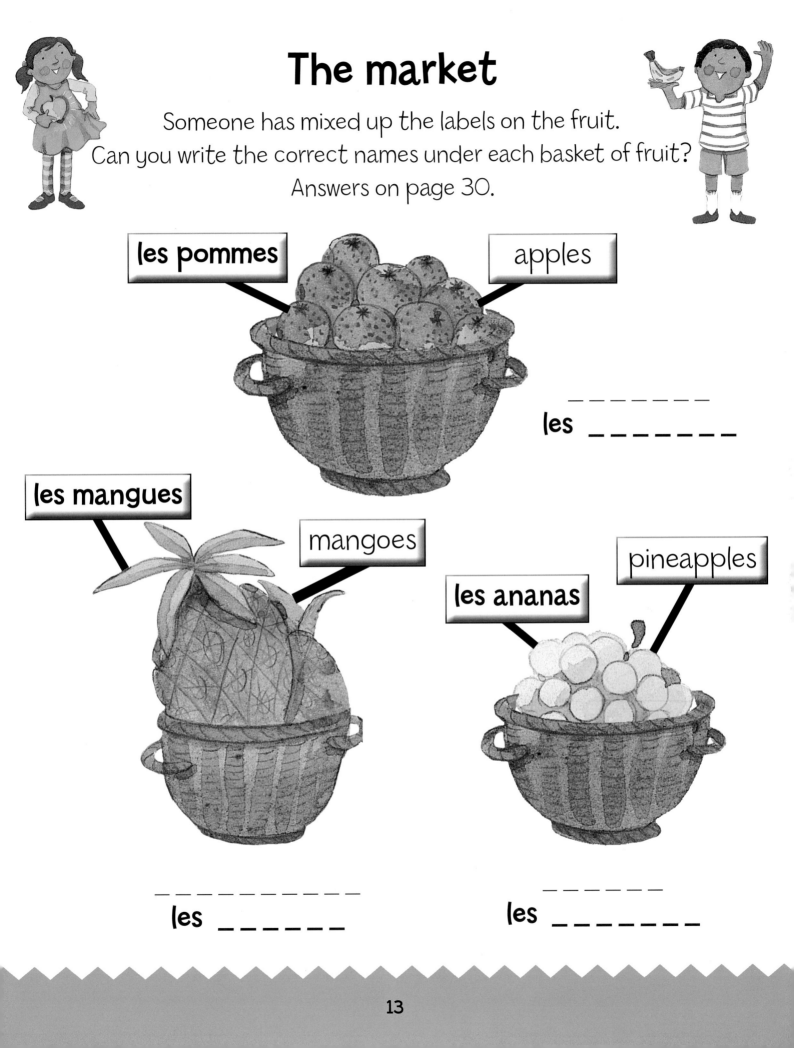

les pommes

apples

les _ _ _ _ _ _ _ _

les mangues

mangoes

les ananas

pineapples

les _ _ _ _ _ _ _

les _ _ _ _ _ _ _ _

Dans la forêt

Complète les mots. Commence par la lettre entourée dans la grille et va vers le haut, vers le bas ou sur le côté pour trouver le nom de ces neuf animaux et insectes. Solutions à la page 31.

de_ _
le _ _rf

_q _ i _ re _
l'é_ _re_ _l

l	l	o	n	c	x	h	m
i	i	p	z	h	e	n	f
p	n	a	o	s	w	i	l
a	c	l	n	u	r	d	l
p	e	m	f	d	b	o	e
e	r	z	e	i	s	w	r
é	f	s	o	u	r	m	e
b	é	d	f	d	r	a	n
a	c	u	r	e	u	i	w
r	z	o	m	d	s	l	e
a	i	w	o	f	e	m	z
c	s	e	h	c	u	o	f

bu _ t _ rf _ _
le p_ _il_on

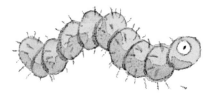

ca _ e _ p _ _ l _ r
la _he_il_ e

14

In the forest

Fill in the missing letters. Find the names of these nine animals and insects starting at the circled letter and going up, down, and sideways. Answers on page 31.

x	c	a	t	t	e	r	p	u
t	y	b	a	s	o	d	i	n
f	l	b	r	z	k	f	l	l
r	w	i	r	a	e	b	c	a
e	f	t	a	n	o	n	v	r
t	n	d	n	d	f	w	l	f
t	o	e	s	b	r	o	r	o
u	r	e	l	n	c	s	d	x
b	x	r	s	q	u	i	r	s
e	h	a	w	c	o	a	r	o
l	d	f	n	a	d	f	e	a
t	e	e	b	y	l	f	l	w

_ _ x
le _ e _ ar_

br_w_ b_ _ r
l'_ur_ _r_n

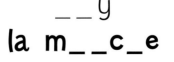

_ _ y
la m_ _ c_ e

b_e_ _e
le _ _ar_b_ _

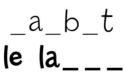

_ a_b_t
le la_ _ _

Dans la chambre

Complète les mots. Ensuite fais les mots croisés
et vérifie les réponses à la page 31.

al_ _m cl_c_
le ré_ _i_

r_g
le ta_i_

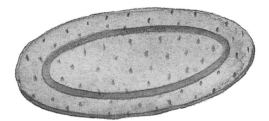

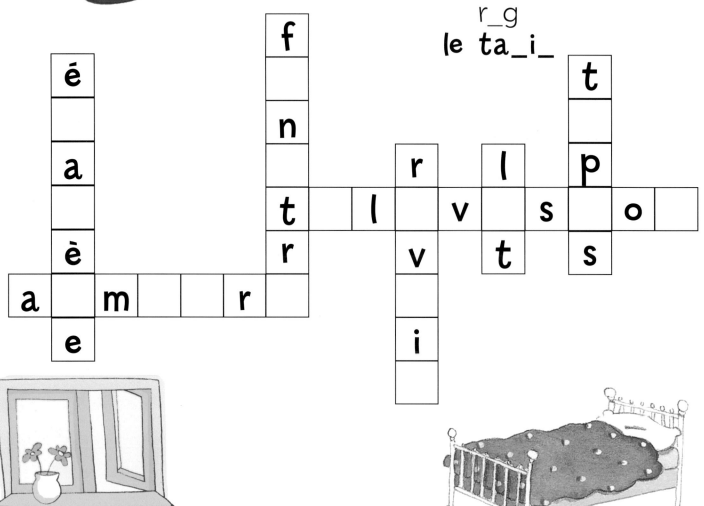

wi_d_ _
la f_ _ê_r_

b_d
le l_ _

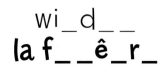

16

In the bedroom

Label the pictures. Then fill in the crossword
and check your answers on page 31.

s_e_f
l'é_a_è_e

w_r_r_ _ _
l'a_m_i_e

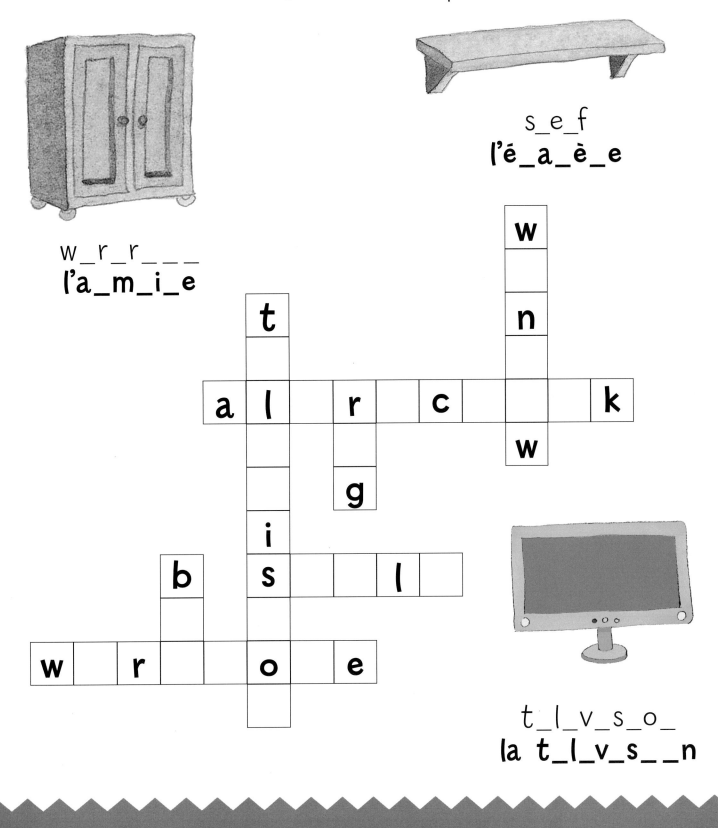

t_l_v_s_o_
la t_l_v_s_ _n

Les nombres et les mois

Ecris le numéro sur le calendrier. Ensuite relie chaque calendrier au bon mois. Solutions à la page 31.

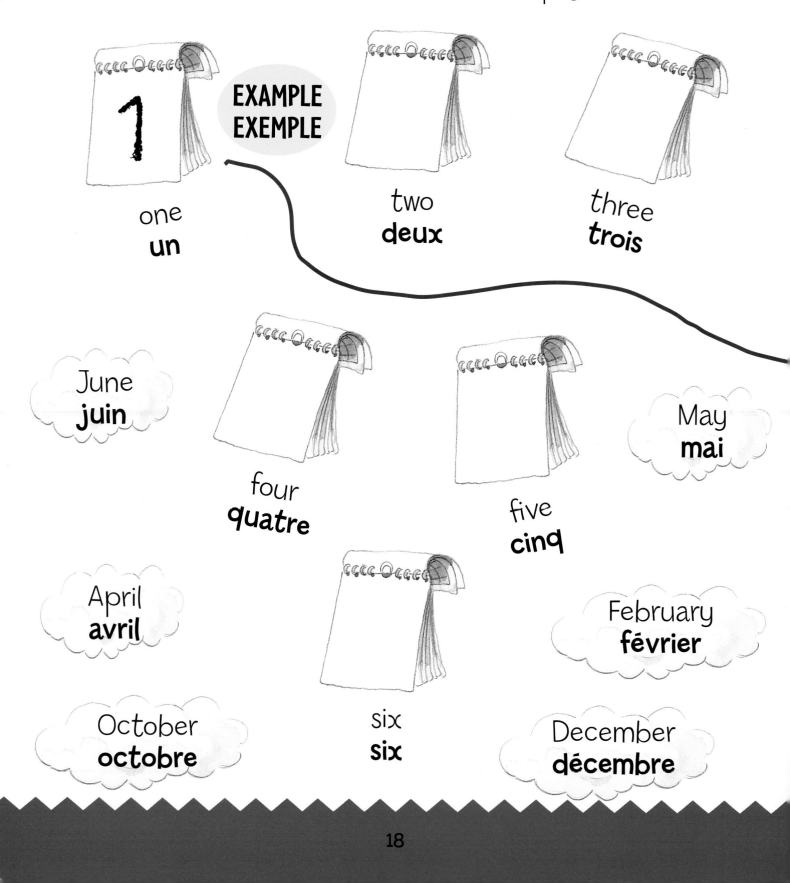

EXAMPLE
EXEMPLE

1

one
un

two
deux

three
trois

June
juin

four
quatre

five
cinq

May
mai

April
avril

February
février

October
octobre

six
six

December
décembre

Numbers and months

Fill in the number on the calendar. Then join each calendar to the right month. Answers on page 31.

July
juillet

seven
sept

eight
huit

August
août

January
janvier

nine
neuf

ten
dix

eleven
onze

September
septembre

March
mars

twelve
douze

November
novembre

Les vêtements

Complète le nom des vêtements.
Ensuite trouve ces neuf mots dans
la grille. Solutions à la page 31.

s_i_t
la j_p_

d_e_s
la r_b_

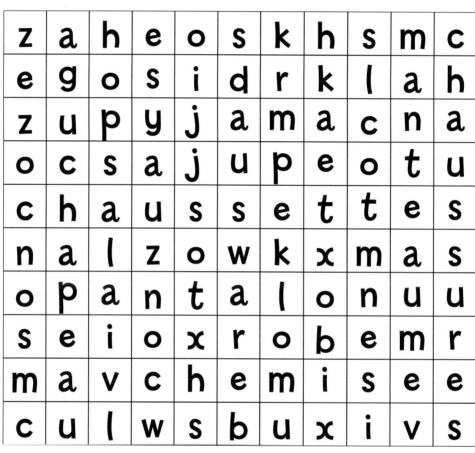

z	a	h	e	o	s	k	h	s	m	c
e	g	o	s	i	d	r	k	l	a	h
z	u	p	y	j	a	m	a	c	n	a
o	c	s	a	j	u	p	e	o	t	u
c	h	a	u	s	s	e	t	t	e	s
n	a	l	z	o	w	k	x	m	a	s
o	p	a	n	t	a	l	o	n	u	u
s	e	i	o	x	r	o	b	e	m	r
m	a	v	c	h	e	m	i	s	e	e
c	u	l	w	s	b	u	x	i	v	s

c_a_
le m_n_e_u

s_o_s
les c_a_s_u_e_

p_j_m_s
le p_j_m_

Clothes

Find the nine words in the puzzle using the picture clues.
Answers on page 31.

s _ c _ s
les c _ a _ s _ e _ t _ s

s _ i _ t
la c _ e _ i _ e

s	r	a	n	o	t	w	d	j	e
k	x	u	a	i	k	s	l	d	r
i	c	w	r	s	h	o	e	s	t
r	l	e	c	q	r	s	f	o	g
t	m	d	o	i	e	w	z	c	d
p	a	j	a	m	a	s	e	k	r
c	s	u	t	o	i	h	k	s	e
d	e	f	s	a	z	i	w	o	s
t	r	o	u	s	e	r	s	c	s
a	d	z	x	h	a	t	v	e	k

h _ t
le _ h _ p _ a _

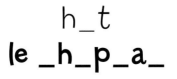

t _ o _ s _ r _
le pa _ t _ l _ n

21

Dans la salle de classe

Numérote chaque lettre de l'alphabet de 1 à 26.

Exemple: **19 1 12 12 5   4 5   3 12 1 19 19 5** = **salle de classe**.

Ensuite décode ces mots. Solutions à la page 31.

3	8	1	9	18

20	1	2	12	5

12	1		3	8	1	9	19	5

12	1		20	1	2	12	5

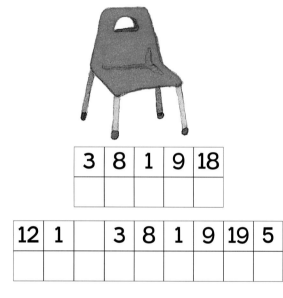

2	15	15	11

12	5		12	9	22	18	5

3	15	12	15	18		16	5	14	3	9	12

12	5		3	18	1	25	15	14		4	5		3	15	21	12	5	21	18

20	5	1	3	8	5	18

12	1		13	1	9	20	18	5	19	19	5
					^						

a b c d e f g h i j k l m

In the classroom

Number each letter in the alphabet from 1-26. For example, **classroom** is **3 12 1 19 19 18 15 15 13**. What are the names of these things in the classroom? Answers on page 31.

7	12	21	5

12	1		3	15	12	12	5

16	1	16	5	18

12	5		16	1	16	9	5	18

16	5	14

12	5		19	20	25	12	15

3	15	13	16	21	20	5	18

12		15	18	4	9	14	1	20	5	21	18
	,										

n   o   p   q   r   s   t   u   v   w   x   y   z

À la plage

Suis les lignes et récris les mots. Ensuite utilise les lettres entourées pour trouver les mots qui manquent en bas de la page 25. Solution à la page 31.

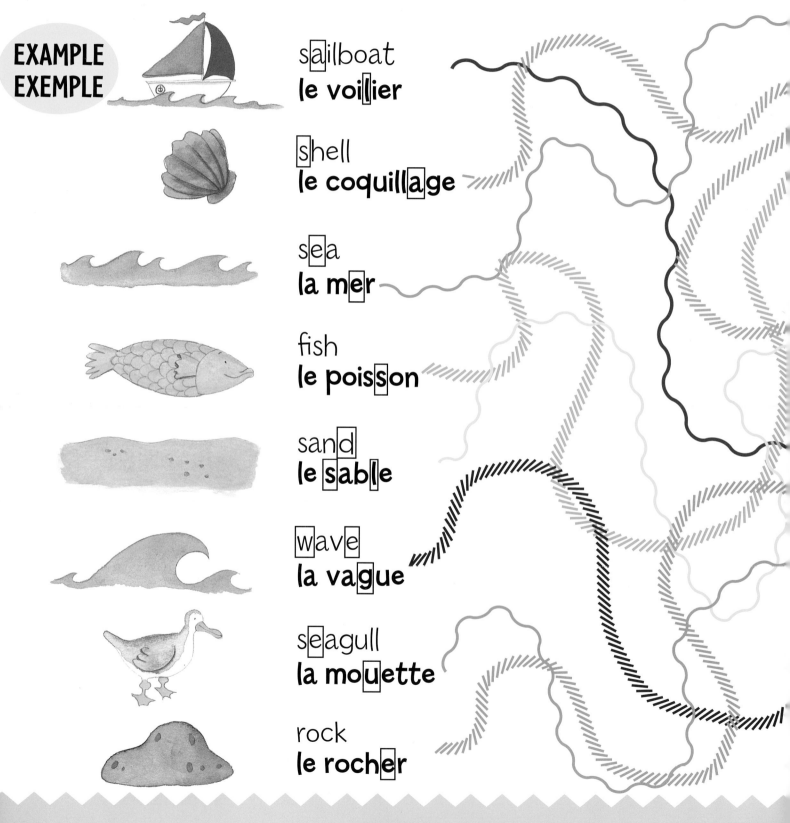

EXAMPLE EXEMPLE

sailboat
le voilier

shell
le coquillage

sea
la mer

fish
le poisson

sand
le sable

wave
la vague

seagull
la mouette

rock
le rocher

At the seashore

Follow the tracks and rewrite the words. Use the letters in boxes to make words for the final missing labels at the bottom of page 25.
Answer on page 31.

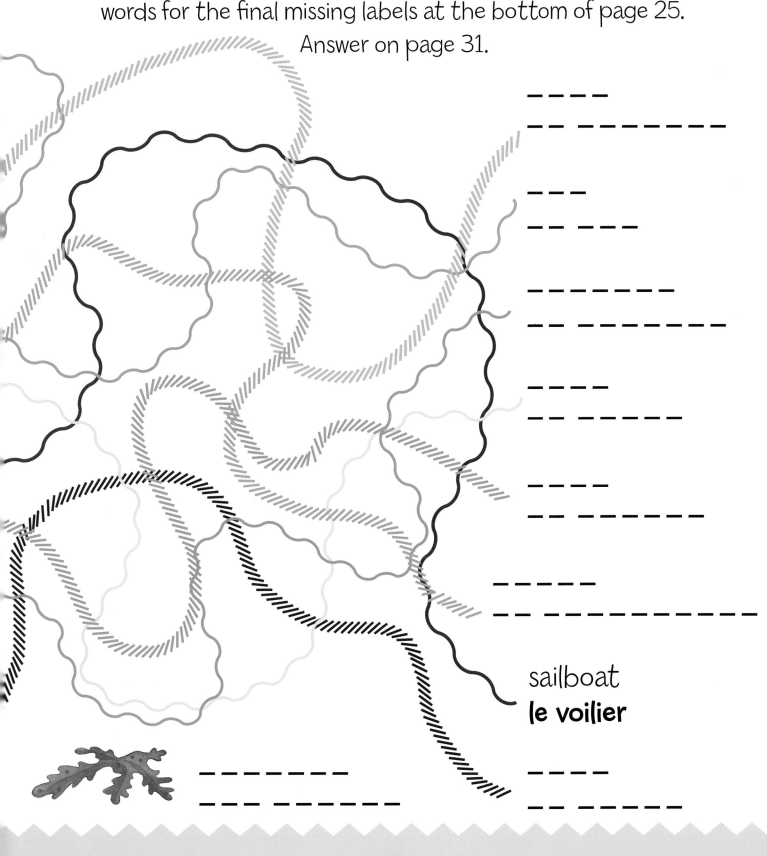

_ _ _ _

_ _ _ _ _ _ _ _ _

_ _ _

_ _ _ _ _

_ _ _ _ _ _ _

_ _ _ _ _ _ _ _

_ _ _ _

_ _ _ _ _ _ _

_ _ _ _

_ _ _ _ _ _ _ _

_ _ _ _ _

_ _ _ _ _ _ _ _ _ _ _ _

sailboat
le voilier

_ _ _ _ _ _

_ _ _ _ _ _ _ _

_ _ _ _

_ _ _ _ _ _

Les légumes

Trouve le nom des légumes dans le serpentin et complète les mots. Solutions à la page 31.

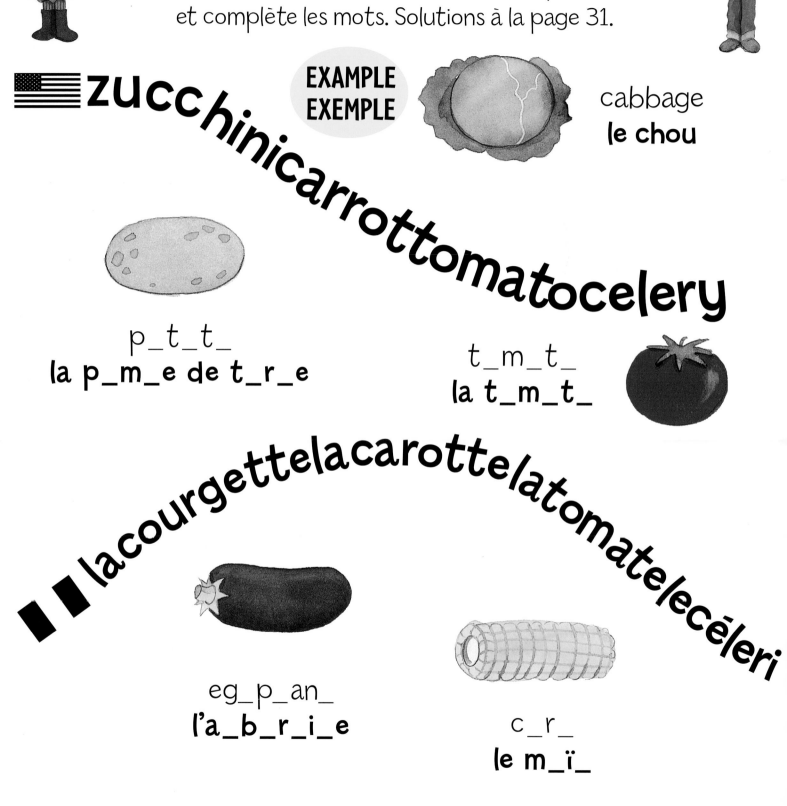

zucchinicarrottomatocelery

EXAMPLE
EXEMPLE

cabbage
le chou

p_t_t_
la p_m_e de t_r_e

t_m_t_
la t_m_t_

lacourgettelacarottelatomatelecéleri

eg_p_an_
l'a_b_r_i_e

c_r_
le m_ï_

Vegetables

Find the names of the vegetables in the word snake to complete their labels. Answers on page 31.

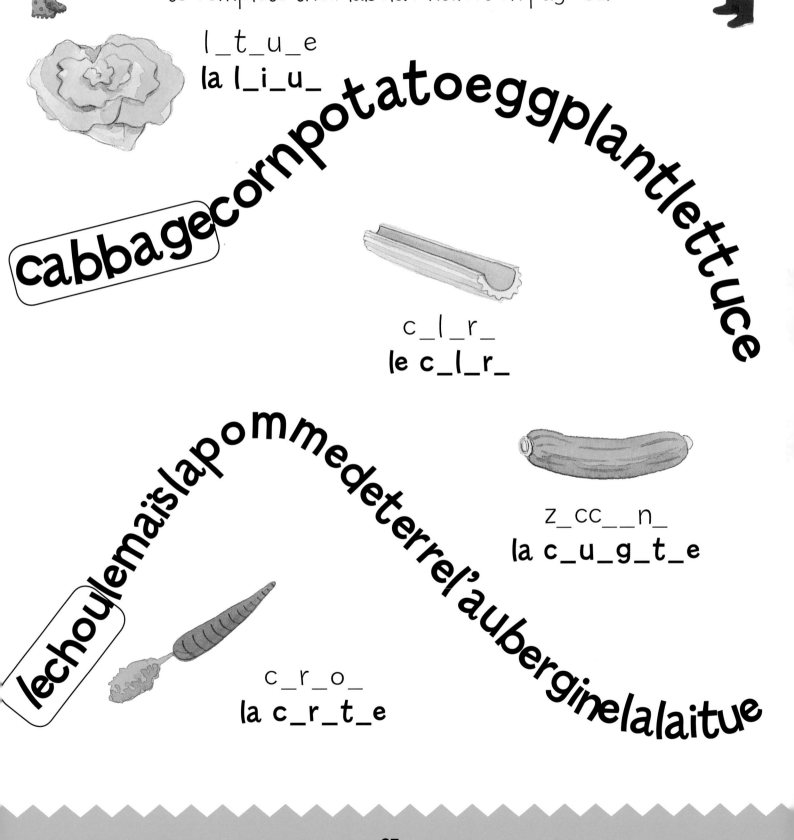

l_t_u_e
la l_i_u_

cabbagecornpotatoeggplantlettuce

c_l_r_
le c_l_r_

lechoulemaïslapommedeterrel'auberginelalaitue

z_cc__n_
la c_u_g_t_e

c_r_o_
la c_r_t_e

À la campagne

Trouve les neuf différences entre les deux dessins.
Les indices ci-dessous sont à l'envers. Récris-les correctement
pour trouver les différences. Solutions à la page 31.

1. niatnuom   mountain
   engatnom al   **la montagne**

2. rewolf   _ _ _ _ _ _
   ruelf al   _ _ _ _ _ _

3. egdirb   _ _ _ _ _ _
   tnop el   _ _ _ _ _ _

4. kcud   _ _ _ _
   dranac el   _ _ _ _ _ _ _

5. eert   _ _ _ _
   erbra l'   _ _ _ _ _ _

In the country

Spot the nine differences between the two pictures.
The clues below are back to front. Rewrite them to
help you find the differences. Answers on page 31.

6. drib _ _ _ _
   uaesio l' _ _ _ _ _ _ _

7. tibbar _ _ _ _ _ _
   nipal el _ _ _ _ _ _ _

8. dleif _ _ _ _ _
   pmahc el _ _ _ _ _ _ _

9. ssarg _ _ _ _ _
   ebreh l' _ _ _ _ _ _

Solutions/Answers

p.2

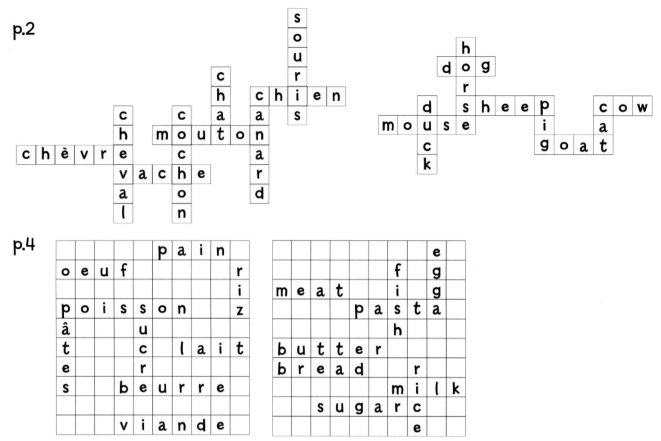

p.4

(crossword grids)

Grid 1:
- pain
- oeuf / riz
- poisson
- âtes / our / lait
- es / c / r
- s / beurre
- viande

Grid 2:
- egg
- fig
- meat / fish
- pasta
- h
- butter
- bread / r
- milk
- sugar / ce

p.6 – cat/**le chat**, butterfly/**le papillon**, snake/**le serpent**, elephant/**l'éléphant**, giraffe/**la girafe**, crocodile/**le crocodile**, tiger/**le tigre**, hippopotamus/**l'hippopotame**

p.8 – sink/**l'évier**, saucepan/**la casserole**, spoon/**la cuillère**, fridge/**le frigo**, glass/**le verre**, plate/**l'assiette**, stove/**la cuisinière**, fork/**la fourchette**, knife/**le couteau**

p.10

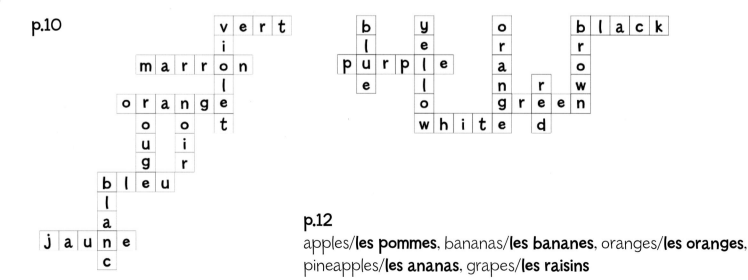

p.12
apples/**les pommes**, bananas/**les bananes**, oranges/**les oranges**, pineapples/**les ananas**, grapes/**les raisins**

p.14

l	l	o	n	c		
i	i	p		h	e	n
p	n	a			i	l
a	c	l	n	u	r	
p	e			b		e
e	r			s		r
é	f	o	u	r		e
b	é		d	r	a	n
a	c	u	r	e	u	i
r				l		
a				m		
c	s	e	h	c	u	o

	c	a	t	t	e	r	p
		y	b	a			i
f	l	b	r			l	l
r	i	r	a	e	b		a
e	t				n		r
t	d				w		f
t	e			b	r	o	o
u	e						x
b	r	s	q	u	i	r	
e						r	
l						e	
t	e	e	b	y	l	f	l

p.16

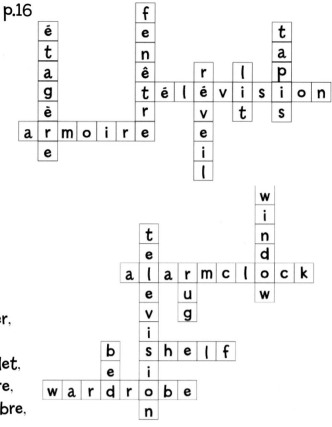

p.18 – one/**un**-January/**janvier**, two/**deux**-February/**février**, three/**trois**-March/**mars**, four/**quatre**-April/**avril**, five/**cinq**-May/**mai**, six/**six**-June/**juin**, seven/**sept**-July/**juillet**, eight/**huit**-August/**août**, nine/**neuf**-September/**septembre**, ten/**dix**-October/**octobre**, eleven/**onze**-November/**novembre**, twelve/**douze**-December/**décembre**

p.20

							m	c		
							a	h		
		p	y	j	a	m	a	n	a	
	c			j	u	p	e	t	u	
c	h	a	u	s	s	e	t	t	e	s
	a						a	s		
P	a	n	t	a	l	o	n	u	u	
	e			r	o	b	e	r		
	a		c	h	e	m	i	s	e	e
	u						s			

s									
k									
i			s	h	o	e	s		
r		c				s	o		
t		o				c	d		
P	a	j	a	m	a	s	k	r	
	t				h	s	e		
					i	s			
t	r	o	u	s	e	r	s	s	
	h	a	t						

p.22 – chair/**la chaise**, table/**la table**, book/**le livre**, color pencil/**le crayon de couleur**, teacher/**la maîtresse**, glue/**la colle**, paper/**le papier**, pen/**le stylo**, computer/**l'ordinateur**

p.25 – seaweed/**les algues**

p.26 – potato/**la pomme de terre**, tomato/**la tomate**, eggplant/**l'aubergine**, corn/**le maïs**, lettuce/**la laitue**, celery/**le céleri**, zucchini/**la courgette**, carrot/**la carotte**

p.28 – mountain/**la montagne**, flower/**la fleur**, bridge/**le pont**, duck/**le canard**, tree/**l'arbre**, bird/**l'oiseau**, rabbit/**le lapin**, field/**le champ**, grass/**l'herbe**

Vocabulaire/Word list

les algues seaweed
l'ananas pineapple
août August
l'arbre tree
l'arc-en-ciel rainbow
l'armoire wardrobe
l'assiette plate
l'aubergine eggplant
avril April
la banane banana
le beurre butter
blanc/blanche white
bleu/bleue blue
la campagne country
le canard duck
la carotte carrot
la casserole saucepan
le céleri celery
le cerf deer
la chaise chair
la chambre bedroom
le champ field
le chapeau hat
le chat cat
les chaussettes socks
les chaussures shoes
la chemise shirt
la chenille caterpillar
le cheval horse
la chèvre goat
le chien dog
le chou cabbage
cinq five
le cochon pig
la colle glue
le coquillage shell
les couleurs colors
la courgette zucchini
le couteau knife
le crayon de couleur color pencil
le crocodile crocodile
la cuillère spoon
la cuisine kitchen
la cuisinière stove
le dauphin dolphin
décembre December
deux two
dix ten
douze twelve

l'écureuil squirrel
l'éléphant elephant
l'étagère shelf
l'évier sink
la fenêtre window
la ferme farm
février February
la fleur flower
la forêt forest
la fourchette fork
le frigo fridge
les fruits fruit
la girafe giraffe
l'herbe grass
l'hippopotame hippopotamus
huit eight
janvier January
jaune yellow
juillet July
juin June
la jupe skirt
le lait milk
la laitue lettuce
le lapin rabbit
les légumes vegetables
le lit bed
le livre book
mai May
le maïs corn
la maîtresse teacher
la mangue mango
le manteau coat
le marché market
marron brown
mars March
la mer sea
le mois month
la montagne mountain
la mouche fly
la mouette seagull
le mouton sheep
neuf nine
noir/noire black
le nombre number
novembre November
octobre October
l'œuf egg
l'oiseau bird
onze eleven

l'orange orange (fruit)
orange orange (color)
l'ordinateur computer
l'ours brun brown bear
le pain bread
le pantalon trousers
le papier paper
le papillon butterfly
les pâtes pasta
la plage beach
le poisson fish
la pomme apple
la pomme de terre potato
le pont bridge
le pyjama pajamas
quatre four
les raisins grapes
le renard fox
le réveil alarm clock
le riz rice
la robe dress
le rocher rock
rouge red
le sable sand
la salle de classe classroom
le scarabée beetle
sept seven
septembre September
le serpent snake
six six
la souris mouse
le stylo pen
le sucre sugar
le supermarché supermarket
la table table
le tapis rug
la télévision television
le tigre tiger
la tomate tomato
trois three
un one
la vache cow
la vague wave
le verre glass
vert/verte green
les vêtements clothes
la viande meat
violet/violette purple
le voilier sailboat